I0040310

Remarkable Business

Spotlights on Top Professionals and Business Owners

.

Remarkable Business

Spotlights on Top Professionals and Business Owners

Leading Professionals and Business Owners

Featuring:

John Patrick

Adam Marburger

Randy Wildman Brown

Dale Cooper

Lisa W. Beckwith

Emmeline Craig

Shawn Yesner

Mary Ellen Ciganovich

Giselle Mascarenhas

Marsha Terry

Remarkable Press™

Royalties from the retail sales of **"REMARKABLE BUSINESS: SPOTLIGHTS ON TOP PROFESSIONALS AND BUSINESS OWNERS"** are donated to the Global Autism Project:

AUTISM KNOWS **NO BORDERS;**
FORTUNATELY NEITHER DO WE.®

The Global Autism Project 501(C)3 is a nonprofit organization that provides training to local individuals in evidence-based practice for individuals with autism.

The Global Autism Project believes that every child has the ability to learn, and their potential should not be limited by geographical bounds.

The Global Autism Project seeks to eliminate the disparity in service provision seen around the world by providing high-quality training to individuals providing services in their local community. This training is made sustainable through regular training trips and contiguous remote training.

You can learn more about the Global Autism Project and make direct donations by visiting **GlobalAutismProject.org.**

Copyright © 2021 Remarkable Press™

All rights reserved. No part of this publication may be reproduced, distributed, or transmitted in any form or by any means, including photocopying, recording, or other electronic or mechanical methods, without the prior written, dated, and signed permission of the authors and publisher, except as provided by the United States of America copyright law.

The information presented in this book represents the views of the author as of the date of publication. The author reserves the right to alter and update their opinions based on new conditions. This book is for informational purposes only.

The author and the publisher do not accept any responsibilities for any liabilities resulting from the use of this information. While every attempt has been made to verify the information provided here, the author and the publisher cannot assume any responsibility for errors, inaccuracies, or omissions. Any similarities with people or facts are unintentional.

Remarkable Business/ Mark Imperial —1ˢᵗ ed.

Managing Editor/ Shannon Buritz

ISBN: 978-1-954757-02-8

CONTENTS

A NOTE TO THE READER

Thank you for buying your copy of "REMARKABLE BUSINESS: Spotlights on Top Professionals and Business Owners." This book was originally created as a series of live interviews; that's why it reads like a series of conversations, rather than a traditional book that talks at you.

I wanted you to feel as though the participants and I are talking with you, much like a close friend or relative, and felt that creating the material this way would make it easier for you to grasp the topics and put them to use quickly, rather than wading through hundreds of pages.

So relax, grab a pen and paper, take notes, and get ready to learn some fascinating Remarkable Business strategies.

Warmest regards,

Mark Imperial
Publisher, Author, and Radio Personality

INTRODUCTION

"REMARKABLE BUSINESS: Spotlights on Top Professionals and Business Owners" is a collaborative book series featuring leading professionals from across the country.

Remarkable Press™ would like to extend a heartfelt thank you to all participants who took the time to submit their chapter and offer their support in becoming ambassadors for this project.

100% of the royalties from this book's retail sales will be donated to the Global Autism Project. Should you want to make a direct donation, visit their website at GlobalAutismProject.org

JOHN PATRICK

JOHN PATRICK

Conversation with John Patrick

Tell us about your business and the people you specialize in helping.

John Patrick: We were founded in 2008 after I exited the banking industry after 30 years. The real focus is on helping clients who have hit milestones that seem to stop a business. We've determined through the years that very predictable things are going to happen after hitting certain milestones. In that case, we help clients identify what is getting in the way and moving it out of the way. It can be anything from the concept to the exit or sale of the company.

We have worked with one-person solopreneurs and with Fortune 50 companies and many companies in between. No matter how small or large the client, we live by our mission statement that "Each business owner, executive, employee, vendor or customer/client we interact with is left transformed in such a way that they see all new possibilities that they never imagined before - for themselves, their company, their family and for the world." It's not transactional; it's transformational.

How has the recent pandemic affected your business?

John Patrick: I personally work in two areas, one in which I spend a lot of time inside the business, picking it apart, and identifying where some systems or processes need to be put into place. So the first thing that changed for me was not being able to be there physically. I had to pivot to somewhat virtual and move our business model outside of that until it is safe to be back in the actual office spaces.

The other side is that I work with companies who got to a point where they, unfortunately, had to file Chapter 11 Bankruptcy. I help them reorganize the company to exit back stronger than they ever were with the idea that they can now be a thriving company. Additionally, the court systems were all closed down. So, as a result, it was just a matter of stepping back and listening to the market. One of the things I identified early on is some of the most well-respected companies started during a period where there was a significant issue around the economy. These include Netflix, Microsoft, GE, and Trader Joe's. They were faced with very similar problems that we are experiencing as a result of the pandemic. For me, it has been about attracting that, and I am as busy or busier than I was pre-COVID. It has allowed people to take stock and take the time to get creative. As a result, we've launched several new companies in the midst of all of this. Now that we are starting to get together in person again, I can sit down with my clients over a cup of coffee and help them create something.

What are the new priorities of people reaching out to you?

John Patrick: Many are cash flow related. Sales are down, and they have been forced to close or revamp their business. They question whether they have a viable business and if they are going to be able to continue. In those cases, I'm able to just sit down with them and work through where they can save money. While historically, I haven't done that, I negotiated significant debt reduction where they can now manage based on the new cash flow.

The other part, which keeps me up at night, is that many people have just withdrawn and are now feeling isolated. They have stopped selling and stopped doing what really would help them be prepared on the other side. Part of that is to create what the future would look like by dealing with today and understanding that this too shall pass. And when it does, we will come out even stronger and more streamlined than ever before.

Can you share some of the new launches and opportunities that have come about due to the pandemic?

John Patrick: I have one particular business that is creating a cremation garden, which is a very unique, one of a kind niche. There is a whole history and a study around the scattering of ashes, which is harmful to the ground and plant life. So they created a process where they're able to make it eco-friendly. They are making a destination for families to come to in the form of a beautiful garden, and it is part of a very historical cemetery. Another client started with the concept of creating a little mom and pop Asian and Latin market. That has turned into us putting an offer into buying a company and focusing on growing that business. For a third client, we used the downtime to create all documentation and processes to take the company to the franchise model. Those are the three big ones right now, all while helping others along the way to get their concept down.

You mentioned helping business owners to identify specific milestones. Can you tell us a little about that and what some of these milestones are?

John Patrick: I don't know if there has been anything published regarding this, but specific laws are in effect in life. One of them is the 80/20 rule, where 80% of the work is done by 20% of the people, or 80% of the profit comes from 20%

of what you do. I have a law I refer to as the "law of ones and threes." Let's use revenue as an example. If a company's revenue starts with a three, such as $300,000, and they want to move it to a number that begins with a one, such as $1 million, significant changes have to be made. You may be doing $300,000 all on your own, but you will need a team in place to reach $1 million. Once you want to move from $1 million to $3 million, you need to incorporate a structure. And then, from $3 million to $10 million, it makes sense to start automating the process, developing a board of directors, and turning the control of the business over to someone else. At each step along the way, I can have a conversation with a client or prospective client, and in five minutes, I can tell them where the revenue is because of what they're dealing with. Once they get over the shock of that, it's very predictable, and we can focus on what we have to do to get to the next level.

As you talk about scaling a business, does it come down to the business owner's personal preference? Or is there a way to determine what size the company should be? Do you often come across people that just want to stay small?

John Patrick: Absolutely. One of my clients is acquiring one of those $3 million revenue companies that should be $10 million. In talking to the owners, they agree that it should be a $10 million company. However, in their case, they chose to make the business a lifestyle business. They don't even pretend otherwise. As long as they had enough money to travel, have fun with the kids, and pay the bills, they were content with that. The new owner coming in is looking at creating a legacy and something of significance. Neither one is more right or wrong than the other; it is merely a preference. One chooses enough money to be comfortable, while the other decides to build an empire.

In my opinion, the size of a company is limited to the vision of the owner, founder, or executive(s), to their penchant or aversion to risk, and in their ability to let go, meaning a willingness to build a team of people around them that supports their vision yet is allowed to move things along.

Is there a specific formula used to scale businesses safely?

John Patrick: This typically comes in the formation of a business plan. Part of that is doing all the market research, looking at what other companies are doing, what the market will support, and all of their margins. Typically, a business plan is about 40 to 50 pages, but this particular business plan was 274 pages. So it was significant. It's not a cut and dry formula, as it is researching the area's competitors. If you put the business at an intersection in a small town with five buildings, it probably couldn't be a $10 million company. And if it was in downtown New York City, it might be a $100 million company. But the market in the area would support it to be $10 million.

What inspired you to get started with Tampa Bay Business Consultants?

John Patrick: I spent 30 years in the banking industry, and while sitting in Puerto Rico at a meeting, I realized that even after 30 years, I didn't have real control over my life. I was only as good as my numbers for the year. I started to evaluate whether I wanted to spend the rest of my life working for "the man," getting my watch and party at the end and moving on. I was presented with an opportunity to run a company and decided this was a perfect time, and it was right before the big financial crash of 2008. So I was able to sell my stock and made a significant amount of money right before it all fell apart. I started a company and ran several different companies at varying capacities. And each time, people would say, "You know, people will pay you money for the experience you have. Even within the bank, you built companies." And the more I thought about it, the more I wanted to do it. So I tried it and found that to be true. I was blessed by having all those years managing under P&Ls and watching the numbers. And I have never looked back. I changed the company's name to be more reflective of the area that I served in 2008. And it's just taken off from there.

What makes you unique?

John Patrick: I think what makes us unique is that we deal with transformation. The first thing we address with any client, despite their size, is culture and brand. We create a mission statement that clearly communicates the difference they make, and everything we build with them supports that. By getting employees to embrace the culture, we affect change. And from there, we build their brand. By brand, I do not mean their logo or advertising gimmick … I mean we influence what others (customers, clients, the public) think and say about them when they are not around.

It sounds like you have the ideal fit for your skillset. You have gained so much experience from not only the banking world but creating and running your businesses. Do you also surround yourself with experts in other fields?

John Patrick: Absolutely. I have a great team. I have creative people that study market trends and develop marketing efforts that get the desired results. I have financial wizards that handle bookkeeping and generate client financials. I have strategic thinkers that know what it takes to launch, grow, sustain, and manage successful businesses. And I have a strong advisory board that includes attorneys, accountants, and bankers who can assist clients where needed. I've pretty much learned to do it all, though my passion is sitting across the table from a business owner, talking about their dreams and what they want the business to look like. I enjoy that personal aspect of business.

What is the number one piece of advice you would give to business owners today who are trying to navigate this uncertain time?

John Patrick: I would say, don't do it alone. It is so easy to feel alone during all of this, especially for business owners who often feel that way regardless of the economy's state. They are the ones who carry the burden home. During this time, reach out, talk to people, work through problems, and understand that there is power in numbers. There is power in brainstorming and working things through. Just don't do it alone.

How do people that could benefit from your expertise find you and connect with you?

John Patrick: Email certainly would work, which is john@tampabaybusinessconsultants.com. You can reach my team or me through our website, tampabaybusinessconsultants.com. I can also be reached directly at 813-609-4509.

JOHN PATRICK

President/CEO

Tampa Bay Business Consultants

John Patrick spent thirty years as an executive with a Fortune 50 company, building companies and divisions within the organization before holding Operations Manager, National Director and CEO roles with several companies as a turnaround expert. In 2012 he utilized his experience and knowledge of building profitable businesses in forming Tampa Bay Business Consultants (TBBC). Located in Tampa Bay, Florida, TBBC serves clients nationwide. TBBC helps business owners from conception to exit, and anywhere in between, while most clients come to TBBC upon hitting predictable milestones and plateaus. He is a published author and sought-after speaker on the subject of sales, leadership, customer experience, operations, and business.

Remarkable Business

In addition to his role as CEO of TBBC, John recently launched Christian Business Leadership Mastermind, which brings business owners and executives together to form faith-based relationships while equipping them to run successful companies. His wife, Amy, is the founder of AP Business Solutions, which offers a suite of services to enable companies to run efficiently and effectively. He has three children and seven grandchildren. When not transforming companies, he enjoys quiet evenings with his wife and their cat, Riley.

WEBSITE: https://www.tampabaybusinessconsultants.com

EMAIL: john@tampabaybusinessconsultants.com

PHONE: 813-609-4509

FACEBOOK: https://www.facebook.com/
TampaBayBusinessConsultantsLLC

LINKEDIN: https://www.linkedin.com/in/thejohnpatrick/

ADAM MARBURGER

ADAM MARBURGER

Conversation with Adam Marburger

Adam, you are a Renaissance man of sorts and a serial entrepreneur with a wide variety of interests. Tell us about that.

Adam Marburger: I live my life in the automotive, real estate, and martial arts industries. I am very passionate about all three, and I'm living my purpose through each one.

Describe your journey over the past couple of years.

Adam Marburger: In 2017, I made the bold decision to walk away from a very safe, comfortable existence; a high salary, pretty good schedule, but I just couldn't grow within the four walls of that business. I've had different callings. After 17 years, I just upped and retired. I put in my resignation and my retirement, and I walked away. I then rebuilt and started all over. Leaving the retail side of automotive, it took me about three years to understand the insurance side that I am on now. And without the real estate holdings that I had, I would have never been able to do that. But it took me three years of fighting, kicking, no sleep, and agony to get back to being extremely profitable today. And looking back, I wouldn't change a thing.

You have diversified into three "buckets," so to speak; automotive, real estate, and martial arts. Did you need that balance to stay afloat? How did you keep all those plates spinning?

Adam Marburger: From a very young age, I've had mentors who taught me to understand multiple income streams. Even when I was on the retail side of automotive, I always had other streams of income. I knew that to get where I wanted to go ultimately, I needed that. Real estate was probably an essential piece. My mentor started telling me to get into rentals and multi-family deals to create cash flow. I followed the steps he showed me, and it paved the way for a comfortable source of income that allowed me to hit the reset button. Lastly, I got into the martial arts stream of income, and I'm currently doing pretty well there. I like the idea of not being dependent on one particular area. What happens if the automotive industry freezes again? What if COVID happens like it did in March and April, and then the dealers stop selling cars? Well, I'm not going to make any money. So I need to then depend on my other streams of income.

Many people choose to dabble in real estate as a side gig, but it sounds like you used it as the primary ignition to get your other businesses going. Tell us about that.

Adam Marburger: I was having lunch one day with my partner, Ali, and we started talking about what we could do with $500,000 cash. Well, what if we bought ten properties? And what if those ten properties rented out at $800 to $1,000 a month? We don't owe anything on them. Could we live on that cash flow? And I started thinking, "Hmmm, that's interesting." I wanted more cash flow than that to live the lifestyle that I ultimately wanted to live. But I liked the idea of having ten houses paid off, bringing $800 to $1000 a click. So that's what put the light bulb over my head years ago. And I started thinking, "Okay, how do I buy these foreclosures, fix them up, and then get them paid off as soon as possible?" Instead of doing the 20 and 30-year loans, I started doing ten-year loans on these deals a long time ago. Then the loans would mature, and now it's all cash. Without my mentor, I wouldn't be where I am in the real estate business. But I'm so thankful that our paths crossed. I started investing in real estate in my 20s, and I just turned 40 two weeks ago.

*When you left your high paying job in the auto-
motive industry, you focused on real estate to get
your base. Then you went back into the automotive industry. What are you doing there currently?*

Adam Marburger: I started working at a car dealership when
I was 18 years old. I was going to college, and I didn't know
what I wanted to do. I worked my way up the ladder and ran
a high volume dealership for a very long time. The reality is,
I was still working for someone else. And I wasn't meant to
work for somebody else; I wanted to work on my terms. So
I found my way into the insurance side of the automotive
industry. My company is currently helping car dealers build
wealth, manage their offshore investments and funds, train
key management, and coach everyone in the dealership to do
more, sell more, be more profitable, and stay compliant. I help
car dealers run their businesses. And on the vendor side, it's
quite profitable. It is also very rewarding because I get to work
hand in glove with these dealers that are friends. They become
partners, and I get to help them grow their dealerships.

*How did you reinvent yourself and get back into
the automotive industry? How quick was it for you
to gain clients and have success in the automotive
space?*

Adam Marburger: First of all, imagine this. I made half a
million bucks for over a decade, didn't worry about bills, and
life was super good. And then flip the switch; it goes to zero.

I have three daughters to take care of, so it was a pretty bold move. At first, most of my friends and family thought I was absolutely bananas. But I was going through some personal issues. So I went out to Sedona, Arizona, for a handful of days in 2017. I tell this story a lot. I went out to the desert to get lost to find myself. I came back a new person, and I had found my purpose, my drive. So I went out and started branding myself on social media. I built my company using social media. 100% of my clients are from social media. Now the painful part is, it didn't start paying until now. Three years ago, I was not making money. And it was brutally difficult. There were days I didn't want to get online. There were days I didn't want to get out of bed. There were days I just didn't want to do anything because it was so hard. But I fought through, I kicked through, and I stayed consistent. And now, my social media branding is paying dividends today. So long story short, it was a brutal three years, but I stayed the course. And now it's paying dividends.

What type of services does your Ascent Dealership Services company provide?

Adam Marburger: We provide the insurance products that the dealerships sell to their consumers. When you buy a vehicle and purchase any type of insurance policy, we provide those policies to the dealers. They offer our products, and we give them coaching and mentoring along with it. These dealers also can hire me as a consultant. So I come in, spend time in your dealership, act as an employee, and work all day for a fee. My company, Ascent Dealer Services, is really great at building wealth for our dealers in the most tax-friendly environments. The insurance products that the consumer purchases at the dealership are subject to profit participation. That means the dealer transfers the risk from the insurance company and takes on the risk but keeps the underwriting profit and investment income. We then help the dealer invest those funds and ensure the highest return on investment. We have a division of actuaries and investment brokers with proven track records of assisting dealers in creating an abundance of wealth. I have some of the best dealer partners in the country. I am blessed beyond measure and will forever be grateful.

How has the current pandemic affected your businesses?

Adam Marburger: It has allowed us to pivot. March was pretty difficult. I think March was an eye-opening experience for all business owners that allowed us to slow down, reflect, and have some gratitude for the way things used to be. But then it allowed us to pivot. I turned my coaching platform into an online virtual platform. Through the pandemic, I wrote a lot of material, structured my online Academy, and started looking into the future. At the end of the day, I can't be in 100 stores at once. But I sure can be using Zoom like you and I are right now. So I started using Zoom differently.

And I put it into our blueprint that we offer our dealers, and it worked out quite well. The pandemic caused me to take a few steps back, but it took me 100 steps forward. So we just pivoted and started using technology a little bit differently. And in our dealerships, dealers began using technology to sell cars because customers didn't want to come into the dealership due to pandemic fears. So how are we going to sell cars? Well, we've got to use technology and bring the car dealership to the consumer.

How hard did the pandemic hit the automotive industry? Are cars still moving?

Adam Marburger: It was brutal in March and April. The faucet completely turned off mid-March. April was a challenging month for everybody. But May just soared. The used car industry is absolutely on fire. The new car industry is doing well. The car business is doing very, very well. This month, we will see what happens with the new restrictions. We are looking at what each state is doing since each one is handling things a bit differently. But everything was going really well until right about now. There is definitely some uncertainty. But the end of the year is typically good for car dealers, especially in December. So we'll see what happens. The forward-thinking dealer that is not afraid to shift their old ways of thinking will be on top. We must find a better way of helping our clients purchase vehicles. We must master the art of bringing the dealership to the customer when the customer simply does not have time to visit the dealership. This applies to sales and service, and we have found that fifty percent of the people would prefer NOT to visit the dealership. With all of that being said, we have spent some time working with dealers on how to sell F&I products to customers that never visit the dealership. We also created an online coaching platform that allows us to be in every dealership in the country every single day. The pandemic has forced dealers and vendors to think differently and outside the box.

You and I share a passion for martial arts. Tell us about that part of your life.

Adam Marburger: When I was in high school, I had a friend who said, "Hey, you need to try kickboxing." I always had been an athlete, but I never did kickboxing. He took me to a studio about half an hour from my house. And I was shocked at how much I didn't know. Everybody thinks they know how to fight. But the reality is, you really don't. If you get into a ring with a pro boxer and you've never boxed before, you're done. So it humbled me, and then I got really involved. I did a couple of kickboxing fights. I did a couple of boxing fights. I took a few years off, and then I found mixed martial arts. I was fascinated with MMA. I did a couple of MMA fights. Then I got really, really involved in the sport of Brazilian Jiu-Jitsu, and I am still very active in the sport today. It's my therapy. I had a dealer text me the other day, and it has been a rough day for both of us. I texted him back a picture of my team and my mats and said, "But here's my therapy." This is where the rest of the world doesn't exist. When you're on those mats, the troubles, worries, complaints, financial issues, and everything else just go away. It's my therapy without question.

Take us back a little bit. What inspired you to get into the automotive industry to begin with?

Adam Marburger: I was working in a restaurant for one of my friends. He used to be a car salesman, and he did very well, but he left to open up this Italian restaurant with his wife. I loved working there. I was 18 years old, graduated high school, and went down to Panama City Beach, Florida, to have a good time with some friends. When I got back, they told me they were closing the restaurant. I said, "What the heck, Gordon? What do you mean you're closing the restaurant?!" He said, "Don't worry; I have a plan for you." So he basically kidnapped me and took me to his dealership. I told all of the dealers I didn't want to sell cars. I was out on that deal. So I asked to work in the service department. I was cleaning up and taking out the trash. I did whatever I was told, and I actually liked that job. From the very beginning, everyone told me I needed to be selling. They said, "Adam, you were put on this Earth to sell." And they finally talked me into it. So I started selling cars at 18 years old. I'm not proud of this, but I dropped out of college. Halfway through college, I had a good GPA, but I just wasn't fulfilled. I saw a bigger vision in sales. I was making really good money. And so I walked away from college. I took my automotive career very seriously at that point. Over 17 years, I've worn almost every hat within a dealership in the retail automotive space. I am absolutely blessed to have been a part of that industry.

If you were talking to your younger self, what would your advice be to him when it comes to success?

Adam Marburger: I would probably tell the younger version of myself to slow down a little bit. Slow down and work on being present. Look at the conversations that we're having, listen just a little more, and don't be so quick to react, which then could cause a situation where we overreact. That's what I would tell my younger self. I was always so "go, go, go." And now, as I've gotten older, even though I still have a lot of energy, I've learned how to slow down, pause, and really connect with people by listening more. Before, I just wanted to give my two cents. I would tell my younger version, "Slow down, my friend. You have to slow down so you can speed up."

ADAM MARBURGER

President/CEO

Ascent Dealer Services-Marburger Investment Group-Alton Family Martial Arts

Adam Marburger is a serial entrepreneur that lives his life in three buckets; automotive, real estate, and martial arts. He is the President and CEO of Ascent Dealer Services, an insurance agency specializing in building wealth for automotive dealers across the country. His tremendous track record in retail automotive landed him the title of "Automotive News 40 under 40" in 2018, and that launched him as one of the most sought after coaches in the industry.

Adam plays the role of President/CEO of the Marburger Investment Group and A2 Investments. These companies focus on residential and commercial real estate. His passion for real estate started in his early 20s, where he met his mentor that paved the way. Today Adam is still acquiring new properties and adding them to his portfolio.

Adam's most recent company is very close to his heart. He owns and operates Alton Family Martial Arts & Fitness, located in Alton, IL. Adam is a Brown Belt in Brazilian Jiu-Jitsu and holds National Champion and six-time World Medalist titles. Adam is undefeated in boxing, kickboxing, and Mixed Martial Arts. Today he is sharing his love for martial arts with his community.

Adam has three little "WHYS" named Ahnalee, Arabelle, and Astyn that he coaches daily to become the best possible versions of themselves. He loves being a father, and that is what motivates him on a daily basis. When Adam is not working or spending time with his girls, you will find him traveling as that is his favorite hobby outside of martial arts.

WEBSITE: www.ascentdealerservices.com www.AltonFMA.com

EMAIL: adammarburger@gmail.com

PHONE: 618-979-9483

FACEBOOK: www.facebook.com/adammarburger

FACEBOOK FAN PAGE:www.facebook.com/adampaulmarburger

INSTAGRAM: @adampmarburger

LINKEDIN: linkedin.com/in/adam-marburger

RANDY WILDMAN BROWN

RANDY WILDMAN BROWN

Conversation with Randy Wildman Brown

Randy, you are a man of many distinctions in Jackson, Mississippi. You are the "2020 Jackson Music Award R&B Disc Jockey of the Year" recipient, as well as the "ZBT (Zydeco, Blues and Trail Ride) Outstanding Radio Personality." Tell us a little bit about your work and the people that you help.

Randy Wildman Brown: I have several different projects going on at this time. My debut CD entitled "Just One More Day" has been out for about a year now. My wife, Janice Delores Lee Adams, or as I call her, Miz Wild, and I are elated over the album's release. Everyone that listens to me on my radio show Tuesday nights on WMPR knows it's me when I use my old saying, "I'll sock it to ya, baby."

My wife and I do an annual project called the "Dog Gone 'Dition" Festival. It takes place in the neighborhood we grew up in, as we are focused on the concept of giving back to the hood. We have live entertainment and giveaways; everything is free and open to the public. This particular event's whole objective is to provide school supplies to the less fortunate children where we grew up and relieve some stress for their parents. Especially during these times, a program like this helps out tremendously.

I have been very busy with my album and the "Dog Gone 'Dition" Festival. Also, I am on WMPR radio every Tuesday night right here in Jackson, Mississippi, from 10:00 pm to 2:00 am. At midnight, I have a roll call that goes about 45 minutes, and I call out the names of listeners tuning in from all across the world who enjoy the show. I play Blues, old school Motown, and occasionally I drop a little country because I realize we are from a diverse society today. You have to reach out to as many people as possible to get your message across musically. I promote clean, good music that has an inspiring message to do something positive in life. I have always had an interest in crossing over from radio personality to live recording artist. It's an ongoing passion of mine, and I just love doing what I do.

How has the recent pandemic affected the "Dog Gone 'Dition" Festival?

Randy Wildman Brown: Since everything was shut down, at first, my wife and I didn't believe we would be able to provide the students with supplies this year. Typically, we obtain a permit from the city and start with a live parade from the local elementary and high schools with marching bands and dance routines. They parade through the neighborhood's heart, and once reaching the area where we have the event, they get to perform and show off their particular areas of expertise.

This year, due to the pandemic, we were unable to have live entertainment and food giveaways. However, by God's grace, my wife and I gave away over 450 backpacks full of supplies to children and their parents. The parents just drove through, and we handed them a bag for each child in the car. As a matter of fact, it may have been 500 backpacks or more. And we consider that a success because that's what the "Dog Gone 'Dition" Festival is all about. When we say we give back to the hood, we want to show the kids that we indeed do that for at least one day, even though we have plans to expand and do other things for the children throughout the year. This was our 10th year, and it was a milestone achievement for us. For the first five years or so, my wife and I would dig into our own pockets and do whatever was necessary to make this event happen on our own. But now, we invite local community leaders, government officials in the area, and even people abroad who believe in the concept of "Giving back to the Hood" and children who are less fortunate. They can provide donations to help us accomplish our goals, and we are a 501(c)(3) entity; thereby, all contributions are tax-deductible. Please feel free to view our website: www.randywildmanbrown.com

to make your donations. No contribution is too small, and all contributions are welcome and appreciated.

How has the recent pandemic affected "Wildman Brown Entertainment, LLC"?

Randy Wildman Brown: Since the recent pandemic, my "entertainment" business has been shut down entirely due to the apparent and necessary constraints of social distancing. Indeed, as praiseworthy as Congress' assistance through the "CARES Act," the allocation of funds has been seemingly distributed disproportionately. I have firsthand knowledge of being denied assistance from the Small Business Loan Program, based upon information seemingly lodged arbitrarily and capriciously within your credit report. The record will clearly show many well-financed organizations took advantage of these loans, thereby leaving small business owners like myself and others similarly situated left out to fend for themselves. Now, at the "Eleventh Hour," the 2nd financial Act of Assistance provided by Congress appears to fall three steps shorter than the initial "CARES Act." Seriously, everyone in all aspects related to the "entertainment" business needs help...NOW!

What inspired you to create the "Dog Gone 'Dition" Festival? It sounds like a great thing for the community, and I would love other people to be inspired to do the same in their neighborhoods.

Randy Wildman Brown: It all started with just a group of us sitting around and talking about how we could help the children in our neighborhood. Things had changed since the times when my wife and I grew up here. We used to walk to school, see the elderly sitting on the porch, and cutting the grass, without all of the negative things that have been injected into the neighborhood now. Things like crime, drugs, and prostitution create a negative connotation surrounding the community. And we still have good parents and good children here. We don't want a few bad apples to ruin the whole bunch and have our children thinking this is a way of life. We wanted to show the children an event that allowed everyone to get together without any drugs or violence on the scene. If everyone is having a nice time, it is a great way to inspire the children to be the best they can be. We also have representatives from the fire department that come out and do lectures and other community leaders that speak directly to the children at this event. It is always a family affair. We have been very successful at expanding the event through donations and seeking other people who share our mission. Everyone is willing to come in and help a less fortunate community. Our goal is to give back positively, not to make money off of what we are doing.

I genuinely applaud you for doing this. The world needs more joyous celebrations. For people who would like to learn more about you or get involved in a "Dog Gone 'Dition" Festival, how can they find you and connect with you?

Randy Wildman Brown: They can find me on Facebook at Randy Wildman Brown. Also, they can check out my website at www.randywildmanbrown.com. You can find more information there on what the "Dog Gone 'Dition" Festival is all about and can donate online as well. Please consider donating. And if you'd like to hear some great old school music and blues, I believe in giving every artist a chance to have their music heard. As an independent artist today, it is difficult to get your music played on the radio. One thing lacking in radio today is personality. Personality has been removed from the radio industry across the board. You can pick up anyone off the street and tell them to run a program. But radio is about reaching out to the community and using the platform to give back to the neighborhood. Tune in to my Tuesday night show on WMPR here in Jackson, Mississippi. You can tune in on the radio or at WMPR901FM.com. Feel free to reach me directly at 601-664-8468.

RANDY WILDMAN BROWN

Radio Personality, Recording Artist, Founder of the "Dog Gone 'Dition" Festival

Randy 'Wildman' Brown (Rander Phillip Adams) is indeed a true Sagittarian~November 23, 1953~who was born on the West side of Jackson, Mississippi in an area known as Washington Addition~"That Dog Gone Dition." He is the son of the late Charlie James and Frances B. Adams with three surviving siblings: Sharon Abston~Coleman, Johnnie Adams, and Lydia B. Adams-Macklin. He attended Emmalee Isable Elementary, Blackburn Jr. High, and Jim Hill High before his 1971 graduation from W. H. Lanier High School as Class President. He attended Tougaloo College in Tougaloo, MS., from 1971-1972. He later attended Jackson State University in Jackson, MS., where he majored in Mass Communications and became an active member of the campus radio station: WJSU/88.5 FM. In 1978, Randy 'Wildman' Brown joined the staff at WYAZ in Yazoo City, MS., and later moved to WQBC in Vicksburg, MS., WOKJ, and WKXI in Jackson, MS.

Today, Randy 'Wildman' Brown demonstrates his vast knowledge and experiences in the broadcast industry every Tuesday night on WMPR, 90.1/FM (Mr. Charles Evers & Ms. Wanda Evers) radio in Jackson, MS., from 10 p.m.-2 a.m. (www.wmpr901fm.com). Moreover, he invites you to visit Tunein.com and search for "The Voice of the Community WMPR/FM-90.1", then click on Listen Live. Notably, Randy 'Wildman' Brown later in life married his childhood sweetheart, Janice Delores Lee-Adams, "aka" Miz Wild, who provides her absolute support and encouragement necessary to be the best he can be. In other words, Janice ("Miz Wild") is the unique divine catalyst of Randy "Wildman" Brown as both husband and artist in all aspects and endeavors of his life today. He promises you that ALL tracks from his debut CD (dedicated to His Wife) "Just One More Day" will offer a positive message with strong, vibrant melodic lines! This debut project CD~"Just One More Day," provides a glimpse of a new and very prominent Artist who shall offer much, much more for many years to come. He wholeheartedly respects and recognizes the dedicated assistance in this debut project provided to him by Ms. Tammi 'SYyMBOL' Killingsworth (Graphics & Printing), the late Harrison 'Cap' Calloway-"Mr. Music" (Arrangements), Forrest 'Juke' Gordon (Gate Studios), Stevie J. (Guitar), Greg Flowers (Guitar), The Late Melvin 'House Cat' Hendricks (Arrangements), Ken 'Polk' Gore (Gore Studios), Janice ("Miz Wild"), and certainly last but not least: "YOU: His Dedicated Listeners and Supporters---whose voice resonates daily saying "Randy 'Wildman' Brown...make it happen"!!!~~"I'll Sock It To You Baby"!!~

WEBSITE: www.randywildmanbrown.com

FACEBOOK: https://www.facebook.com/randywildmanbrown

PHONE: 601.664.8468 or 601.940.8917

DALE COOPER

DALE COOPER

Conversation with Dale Cooper

Dale is the founder of Xact Communications, based out of Lexington, Kentucky. Tell us about your business and the people you specialize in helping.

Dale Cooper: We target small to medium businesses. And the reason for that, honestly, is that there's a big void out there. Technology keeps getting tougher and more challenging for average people to be able to sort through. We developed an ecosystem that handles all small to medium business technology and delivers it to the owners. Our mantra is, "You do what you do best. And we'll do what we do best."

What specific types of technology do you specialize in?

Dale Cooper: Everything we do is through the cloud, which is how we service our clients nationwide. We set up in Lexington and can repair and monitor everything from here. We handle unified communications, disaster recovery, backup, managed internet, managed firewall, cybersecurity products, email, server hosting, and virtual desktops.

What makes Xact different?

Dale Cooper: Even though we have grown and plan to grow, even more, we still run our company as a small business. You can reach people you need, including me, very easily!

How has the recent pandemic affected your business?

Dale Cooper: We're considered an essential provider. We never had to close our office. Most of the businesses we serve already provide their employees the option to work from home. Some people take advantage of that, and some don't. But when the pandemic hit, every business wanted to know how to get their employees working from home. For the first 30 to 60 days, we were swamped with service tickets to move everybody home. Moving them wasn't the hard part. It was all about moving them and still ensuring that business could be done securely.

Small businesses are struggling, and many won't make it if they continue to do business the same way they have in the past. Today we can help small businesses compete with large or online businesses! They have to change the approach and embrace technology, and we can make that easy for them!

Are your clients looking to stay at home permanently? Or do you think they will eventually go back to working from their offices?

Dale Cooper: That's a great question. As an initial response, many companies are not reopening their offices. I believe as humans, we are social beings. When I first started some of my businesses, I worked out of my house for years. It is a really tough thing for people when you are locked inside by yourself all the time. Not just for social reasons, but business reasons. Eventually, I think things will smooth out, and we will get that healthy mix back. I have many franchises out west, and I would be taking calls on my cell at midnight because it was still 9:00 pm there. My wife told me to stop giving out my cell number. Let's face it, if you are going to work from home, you can't work 24/7, but that is easier said than done.

How do your customers become aware that they need your services?

Dale Cooper: We have a high closing ratio, probably one of the highest in the industry. Simply, we offer only what they need. Unlike other companies, our customers don't have to put up thousands of dollars upfront. We put that up for them so they can get started very easily with a monthly fee. They may need new computers or a new phone system, and essentially, they are renting those items from us for their monthly fee. And as long as they do that, we can monitor, manage, and repair it and the equipment is always under warranty, so nothing scary will happen. The reality is, businesses know they need cybersecurity and surveillance for internal personnel and insurance risks. Still, they often push these things to the back of their mind because they don't want to deal with them. They also just don't know enough about it. So we bring that expertise to them. They can focus on running their franchise, which is what they do best, while we handle the rest.

How does a brand new business owner get started with you? What does the process look like?

Dale Cooper: If we are working with a franchise, the franchisor typically has a spec sheet or scope of work that we are expected to go by. In a general business case, we start asking questions and simply provide only what they need. We have about 20 different services we can offer, but every customer doesn't need all 20. I have an experienced team of professionals that keep up with the latest technologies and certifications to help our customers make informed decisions.

What inspired you to start Xact Communications?

Dale Cooper: I've been in the telecom industry for 26 years. I saw it changing and knew everything was going to the cloud. So I wanted to get into cloud telecom. Our UCaaS was the first product, and from there, we just listened to our customers. Honestly, I can say we do a great job. We are value-priced, and our customers typically carry over into more and more products based on their needs. We've now moved into offering hardware as a service. Nobody buys PCs anymore. It's all a service. Five years ago, we started that and were on the leading edge, before anyone else, because we listened to our customers. That's what the market needed.

How can businesses that could benefit from Xact Communication services find you and connect with you?

Dale Cooper: You can always call us at 844-YES-XACT or email info@xactcommunications.com. Our website is www.xactcommunications.com. Our goal is not to sell people stuff. We try to provide a solution. Many small businesses have a lot of aches and pains. If we can fix those for them and have it make sense financially, it's a "no-brainer" for everyone involved.

DALE COOPER

Founder, Xact Communications

Dale Cooper is the Founder & CEO of Xact Communications. Dale oversees the day-to-day operations of Xact Communications. Born in rural eastern Kentucky and the first in the family to go to college, he was wired from birth to be an entrepreneur. Dale is a subject matter expert in Telecom Hosted VoIP-TDM, Business Networks & equipment.

He is also responsible for managing the vision and direction with products and key relationships. Dale was the first employee and has grown Xact into a multi-million dollar organization. Xact is based on founding principles of providing the latest managed technology to companies in a single, simplified manner to optimize the customer's businesses. They make the complicated simple for their customers.

Before founding Xact Communications, Dale held various leadership positions, such as Founder and President of eSquared Communications, District Director of Nuvox Communications,

Remarkable Business

District Channel Manager of Nuvox & NewSouth Communications, and President of Galaxy Distributing.

Dale is a 1980 graduate of Eastern Kentucky University with a BBA in Business Administration and obtained his ABA in 1978. In 2019 he received the Distinguished Alumni Award. Dale is a member of the EKU College of Business & Technology Advisor Board.

He is a member of several local associations in Lexington, such as Commerce Lexington and Spark. Dale serves as a mentor to young aspiring entrepreneurs. He is a longtime member of Immanuel Baptist Church in Lexington. Dale is married to Colleen Gaye Cooper and has two adult children, Kevin and Jaclyn.

WEBSITE: www.xactcommunications.com

EMAIL: info@xactcommunications.com

SALES PHONE: 844-YES-XACT

Contact me direct at 859-685-2195 ext 103

LISA W. BECKWITH

LISA W. BECKWITH

Conversation with Lisa W. Beckwith

Lisa, you are the founder of "The L.I.F.E.saving Journey." Tell us about your mission and the people you help.

Lisa W. Beckwith: I am the Founder/CEO of the Ecosystem of L.I.F.E. Lisa W. Beckwith, LLC has a Life Coaching service called The L.I.F.E.saving Journey. This L.I.F.E Coaching Network thrives on presenting services offering individuals the opportunity to see themselves mature by executing a healthy mindset of self-worth, focusing on the individual, executive corporate, and team building spectrums of life. Lisa hopes to inspire kindness, interaction, and active listening tactics while aligning individuals' specific goals and aspirations. She enjoys moving and transcending people in the right direction.

The L.I.F.E.saving Journey" was established in 2018. I put together a program to help people deal with mental illness, inspired by a close family member who experienced some of these issues. I wanted to be a part of helping this community by giving some self-efficiencies and self-love. This program offers wellness to support the mind, body, and soul. We focus on interpersonal and professional issues such as relationships, business decisions, and significant life events. The purpose is to improve their emotional intelligence, interpersonal issues, and career goals starting at 12 weeks and continue it for six, nine, or 12 months. We take a mental and emotional journey to address any type of repressed memories that possibly caused issues in their present life.

What do people want from life coaching?

Lisa W. Beckwith: A life coach will help a person reveal their truth, so they can stop feeling like they do not have a purpose and get the direction they need to enjoy their L.I.F.E.'s journey.

What are some of the most common challenges your clients face?

Lisa W. Beckwith: Well, just balancing life in general, and getting them to a place where goals and wants align, even though it is not currently being executed. I have a system that is "execute," "plan," and "journey." My clients have homework in the form of being ready to transition from where they are to where they want to be. And it can be in any of the elements of life, whether health, finances, spirituality, or relationships. We talk about these elements in our sessions, based upon the individual client's needs.

How can a person become better at what they are doing?

Lisa W. Beckwith: A person can become better in who they are and what they want for their life by being precise and clear with what they want. Then they will have to seek out what matters to them the most with a genuine intention.

What techniques does a life coach offer for a person to not worry?

Lisa W. Beckwith: First, breathe. I know it is a natural thing to do, but sometimes people forget to take deep breaths and focus on what is troubling their spirit. Statistics show that 70% of a person's thoughts are pessimistic. A life coach will help with the thought process to gain control of what they really want. Next, the coach will reinforce techniques that will increase a person's desire to impact a more successful outcome.

Does a life coach help people to have strong self-love?

Lisa W. Beckwith: Absolutely! A life coach can help boost a person's confidence and discover the abilities they never knew they had. A coach will expose positive things for people to see about themselves.

Take us through the process of working with you. What happens when a client first reaches out?

Lisa W. Beckwith: Many times, my clients find me through social media. We'll do an intake by having a brief conversation, and then we will follow up with a written plan. We also want to make sure we are a good fit for one another by going through an assessment. I will ask questions to obtain background information, and then we will proceed with our sessions. Due to COVID, our sessions are currently virtual, but I do have a central office located in the downtown Raleigh area for when things get back to face to face again.

How do you determine if a client is a good fit? What types of people is this great for? And which ones may not be an ideal match for you?

Lisa W. Beckwith: A Life Coach is not a therapist. So if there are medical needs that need to be addressed, I refer the client to a therapist. I am connected with therapists, and we do exchange clients from that standpoint. I determine if someone is a good fit by their answers to the "who, what, when, where, and why" of what they want for themselves. Then we move forward with the plan.

What would stop a person from receiving life coaching?

Lisa W. Beckwith: Great question! When people feel they have accomplished things in their lives, they do not see the need for support. However, a life coach can help a person identify different moods/behaviors that a person could be blinded to by being an active listener. Partnering with someone who is an expert in developing self-awareness will lead them to achieve their professional and personal goals.

What inspired you to become a Life Coach?

Lisa W. Beckwith: Thank you for asking that. I am an author, as well. I just finished my first book entitled, "Food for L.I.F.E.: Lasting Impressions Forever Enjoyed." During that time, my loved one was going through a mental health breakdown, and I asked myself how I could help others without reaching my inner circle first. I wanted this person to feel comfortable with me and not threatened by me because of the role we shared in our lives. Being a Life Coach allows that barrier to be broken down. I desire to help others, but you have to be patient and understand it is a journey, and be willing to take that journey. My passion was established after my book was written and after I saw the trauma of what this condition can do to someone. So I just wanted to help align emotional intelligence and give people the self-confidence they lacked because of a condition or situation in their lives.

Perhaps you could speak out to the audience. What would you say to someone who may be going through challenges and looking for a solution?

Lisa W. Beckwith: I would first thank you personally for allowing me to serve you and offer the opportunity to shift your life. I am a resolution person. That means I have a baseline of wanting to solve the problems and not deal with the problems. I also like to help people move forward in life. And you know, sometimes letting that past go can be a handicap because you're so familiar with it. So given the opportunity to serve, to help a person in their wellness is what I strive to do. I love helping; I love sharing. I know that sharing is caring. And that's something that I enjoy doing to help break the barriers of emotional and cognitive challenges that people are facing.

How can people find you and connect with you?

Lisa W. Beckwith: My website is lisabeckwith.com, and all of my handles are on there. I am a part of Facebook, Instagram, and Twitter. So once you get to that first platform, it will navigate you to the others. My motto is "Life is to serve, and be served."

LISA W. BECKWITH

Founder of "The L.I.F.E.saving Journey"

Wellness Life Coach

Lisa W. Beckwith is the Founder/CEO of the Ecosystem of L.I.F.E Lisa W. Beckwith LLC. The L.I.F.E Coaching Network strives to present services offering individuals the opportunity to see themselves mature by executing a healthy mindset of self-worth, focusing on the individual, executive corporate, and team building spectrums of life. Lisa hopes to inspire kindness, interaction, and active listening tactics while aligning individuals' specific goals and aspirations. Her Literacy Program is called "Transcendent." Lisa's home essentials line is called "Haven & Bloom." The foundation that she is currently working on is called "Be Courageous" (BC). Lisa supports the National Breast Cancer Foundation & St. Jude. She donates to both causes for a cure for cancer.

This establishment ecosystem strives to present services that offer individuals the opportunity to see themselves mature through executing a healthy mind, body, and soul. Lisa's Life Coaching involvement has given her goals to change others' lives through intervention and education..

Lisa is a native of Raleigh, NC. She is a mother of four children and has one grandson. Lisa obtained her bachelor's degree in Business Management from Saint Augustine's University in Raleigh, NC. She is currently earning her master's degree in Elementary Education at the University of Southern California. Lisa is morally driven and feels socially obligated to teach in excellence with compassion and a determined mindset. She is also a Certified Life Coach, obtaining her studies through the Intercontinental Coaching Institute (ICI) program, which establishes itself under the ICF (International Coach Federation) by-laws.

Lisa is the author of two self-help/spiritual books, and two others will be released in 2021. Also, she has two published educational books, and one will be released in 2021. Lisa's guide to life is having a Lasting Impression Forever Enjoyed (L.I.F.E) approach and to live with an optimistic mindset.

WEBSITE: www.lisabeckwith.com

EMMELINE CRAIG

EMMELINE CRAIG

Conversation with Emmeline Craig

Emmeline, you are a fine art painter and a life coach. Tell us about your work and the people you specialize in helping.

Emmeline Craig: I coach both men and women, but mostly women. They are typically already successful in some aspects of their lives but are either feeling like frauds or being unfulfilled on a personal level and not having the life they want. There is unhappiness, no matter what, and it usually comes with a deep-seated lack of self-love. I work a lot on this issue with my clients and it's always wonderful to see how much it changes everything for them.

How did you make the connection from a fine art painter to a life coach?

Emmeline Craig: As a painter, I had some success and opened my own gallery. I had that gallery for eight years. I was present in the gallery two to three days a week, and I met many people there. In parallel to that, I had been doing a lot of self-growth work for years. I was being coached and learning a variety of tools. And I found myself having very deep conversations with my clients, randomly, right off the bat. We would just engage in things that were important for them or me. After that, on numerous occasions, I would receive, much later, sometimes a year or more, an email out of the blue from someone telling me that because of our conversation at my gallery that day, they had taken that step, changed something, dared to go for their dream, dropped the painful relationship, or the soul-crushing job. They shared their story, their victory, with me. That's when I realized that my next step would be a life coach and to help others with what I had learned.

Can you give some examples of common challenges your clients face?

Emmeline Craig: Yes. Sometimes you have a life where you're very busy, and you are getting up every morning doing what you chose to do. You have a job; you have a family; you have all kinds of things on your plate. But you also live in a sort of unease, and you don't know exactly what's going on. And you're often beating yourself up thinking, "Oh my God, with everything that I do and have, I should be happy!" Many people who have very rich lives get to that point where everything they have been building and doing is still not enough, and they are looking for what is wrong. And there is nothing wrong. They just don't have enough time dedicated to work on themselves and connect to what they need to be happy. They are just on a treadmill, and it gets old. When we work together, I create pockets of time for my clients to dig, explore, and contemplate what they want to become from where they are, what they have already accomplished, what feels right, and what is missing. They are willing to dare and take steps to achieve their own inner peace and happiness. We do these calls weekly via video chat. They can create a more significant connection with themselves during our work. They can take stock; they can speak their truth and look at their fears without being judged. They can explore uncharted territories, feel their way into what they want for the future, and move toward it. Finally, they can recognize their true beautiful nature and appreciate who they are, genuinely and unconditionally. And that changes everything for them.

What causes your clients to shift, to change, or improve their lives?

Emmeline Craig: While we work together, they are finally available to themselves on a regular basis. I help them connect with their true power, their unique greatness, and their deep longings, and though the whole work is very much internal, even spiritual in many regards, it affects, in practical ways, their daily life. We create more space, mental space, emotional space, personal care space, explorative space, so they can start creating intentionally instead of reacting to what comes at them. When someone's perception gets larger and shifts, their reality does too.

How long does it take for someone to start turning things around and bring about change?

Emmeline Craig: I usually recommend committing to at least six months of working together because my clients get a lot of clarity and can experience beautiful, durable shifts in such a period, but in fact, a sense of relief and empowerment often shows up early in the process.

What are some mistakes people make that perhaps self-sabotage, leaving them feeling empty or that something is missing in their lives?

Emmeline Craig: We never love ourselves enough. We criticize ourselves very, very quickly. We play old tapes that have been ingrained since we were young. They may not be positive, but we still let them play in the background. Our society glorifies being busy. People never take the time to sit, be quiet, be peaceful, not distracted, not on alert, not multitasking.

They are continually multitasking and not taking the time to feel if they live the life they wish for themselves and whether or not what they do every day fits their wishes. And so they feel the need but aren't really in touch with what they need to know and what they need to do for themselves. In some cases, they know but simply don't make the time. Sometimes they are afraid to upset loved ones or to have to make life-altering changes, so they try to cope and keep going as it is.

Can you give us an example of a transformation that you got to witness in a coaching client?

Emmeline Craig: I met someone at my gallery a few years ago. Despite her past accomplishments, she felt awfully "stuck" in her life, unhappy, unfulfilled, and emotionally raw; she had an eating disorder for decades, avoided social gatherings, and did not know how to change her self-defeating patterns though she wanted to. After nine months of working together, she was going on excursions with groups of strangers, felt happy, took a lot of action on her own, lightened up her relationships with her husband and adult children, and started a volunteer job that she loved. She also let go of her eating disorder. She discovered that she could love herself exactly as she was while becoming who she wanted to be. She became positively radiant and now thoroughly enjoys her life.

What do you want to say to someone who resonates with you but feels wary about coaching?

Emmeline Craig: I'd invite them to have a real conversation with me and to follow their inner guidance. Because if they are unfulfilled now and don't make a move, they might have many regrets down the line. Life is too short to postpone joy.

You mentioned that you came into your work due to the challenges you have overcome in your life. Tell us about those.

Emmeline Craig: I had a very bad genetic bone disease. It made my bones brittle, and I had many fractures in my life, mostly in my youth. I didn't have a normal childhood. I didn't go to school until I was 14 years old and then went on to an adult life filled with more fractures and accidents. I was always beating the odds and doing better than expected. But I was not satisfied, not happy, and looking for love outside of myself. I did not realize how much I needed to appreciate myself. I had not grown up like most kids; I am very small, my body and legs have scars, and I am handicapped, so I was insecure, I did not like myself, and I was looking for love in all the wrong places. I just needed to love myself more, but I was not aware. In 2008 I was diagnosed with breast cancer, and I was out of a marriage that did not work well. That was the beginning of a pivotal shift. I realized I had to change everything in the way I lived my life. So I started with healing.

I began my self-growth deep work with a mentor that is well known in the field, Mary Morrissey. And then from there, I did many programs with people like John Assaraf, Bob Proctor, Rich Litvin, and Steve Chandler, you name them. I invested in all kinds of coaching and self-growth programs, and it really turned my life around. I did the deep-seated work, where I reconciled with who I was regardless of my story. I accepted what happened to me and realized I was not a victim anymore. I took what was there all the time and saw it as a foundation on which to build. I started feeling joyful, free, and confident, like never before.

What inspired you to share what you had learned with others and go into life coaching yourself?

Emmeline Craig: I became so much happier and experienced much more freedom. I quit having a day job, I opened my own art gallery, and I did exclusively what I loved. And it was successful. I felt empowered; I felt lighter. Everything became easier. I fell in love with my life.

How can you get there and not want to share it?

For people who are resonating with your message, how can they reach out and connect with you?

Emmeline Craig: They can get in touch with me and have a conversation without any strings attached. I think relaxed conversations are opportunities for true connection. From there, we can determine if we are a good fit. I'm always available for that. I love conversations, so anyone can feel free to connect with me without being immediately sure that I would be the right coach.

My main website is emmelinecraig.com, where people can see my art and read about my coaching. They can contact me directly from that website. There they can also download a little "ebook of bliss" for free. Alternatively, they can go to artistryoflifecoaching.com to learn more, browse my blog, and read clients' testimonials. If they resonate strongly with any of it, they should follow their intuition and connect with me.

EMMELINE CRAIG

Artist, Life Coach

*Founder of Blissful Gallery and
Artistry of Life Coaching*

Combine a lifelong mastery at beating the odds, a successful career in fine art painting, powerful communication skills, an enormous appetite for life, and you have Emmeline Craig.

Emmeline chose to take on many challenging endeavors in the past two decades, such as reinventing her entire life several times, healing from breast cancer without any chemo or radiation, creating and running her own art gallery for eight joyful years, naming only a few. She's been passionately dedicated to self-growth for more than a dozen years.

She is a talented painter, an ethical business owner, and an inspiring writer, living in a 4'4" tall body.

Her many challenging life experiences gave her unusual perspectives, and she loves to deliver uplifting speeches to light a fire in people.

In addition to her many years in the art business and a rapidly growing career in coaching, Emmeline Craig is also an avid reader, a healthy lifestyle supporter, and a compassionate human rights advocate. Since 2013, she's been contributing to stellar non-profit organizations to protect the planet and repair kids' cleft palates worldwide.

She lives a few miles up the coast from San Francisco and spends her free time watching comedy movies, taking road trips along the Pacific Ocean, or sharing food and conversation with friends.

Ask her how to cook healthy gourmet food in a jiffy, to nourish body and soul. It's her secret talent.

WEBSITES: www.emmelinecraig.com

www.artistryoflifecoaching.com

STUDIO: 415-868-9741

CELL: 415-342-1285

FACEBOOK: https://www.facebook.com/emmeline.craig

LINKEDIN: https://www.linkedin.com/in/emmelinecraig

INSTAGRAM: https://www.instagram.com/craigemmeline/

SHAWN M. YESNER, ESQ

SHAWN M. YESNER, ESQ.

Conversation with Shawn M. Yesner, Esq.

Shawn, you are the Founder of Yesner Law based out of Tampa, Florida. Tell us about your areas of practice and the people you help.

Shawn Yesner: My background is actually on the plaintiff foreclosure side. I was an attorney that worked at what we referred to as a foreclosure mill. I was taking houses away from people and did that for about three years in the early 2000s. The law firm that I was working with actually shut down. So I decided to take what I had learned about doing foreclosures quickly, turn it on its ear, slow down the process, and help people instead. Today, I help homeowners who are in danger of losing their homes due to foreclosure and other similar issues. I help homeowners and borrowers get rid of credit cards, student loans, and IRS debt to get their budget and life back on track.

How has the current pandemic affected your business?

Shawn Yesner: It is interesting because the federal government has put many protections in place, and each state has chosen to put protections in place or not based on what's going on with the pandemic. I see many people that are having trouble making ends meet. I also know many people are on mortgage forbearance plans or student loan forbearance plans, making deals with the IRS and their creditors. But the interesting thing is, I have not yet seen an uptick in foreclosures and bankruptcies, primarily because of the CARES Act and some of the other provisions that the federal government has put in place. It's a fascinating economic debate about whether people can continue to survive and thrive when they're not employed. And how do we as a country, as a local, macro, or micro-economy, begin to dig ourselves out of this? It's a really interesting economic issue, and I don't know that I'm smart enough to come up with any of the answers.

Many people are dealing with mortgage forbearances for the first time. What do people need to know?

Shawn Yesner: The biggest problem with a mortgage forbearance is that it doesn't cure the payment default. All the forbearance does is have you make payments to keep the bank from taking a particular action, like a foreclosure or collection. The biggest issue that people don't understand is that forbearance doesn't fix the payment default. I think we're going to have to pair a forbearance with a loan modification or something similar. Here in Florida, when we had Hurricane Irma three or four years ago, the banks did what they called "streamline modifications." It was a very low or no documentation loan modification. You simply had to show you were impacted in some way by Hurricane Irma. I think countrywide, we're going to have to do something like that to show you were affected by COVID, whether it was getting the virus, losing your job, etc. We need some kind of streamline modification to fix the mortgage arrears as we start to come out on the other side of this. Otherwise, you will have the usual avenues of short selling your house or filing bankruptcy.

The word "forbearance" almost sounds forgiving. Are forbearances damaging to people's credit?

Shawn Yesner: Yes, and no. It's not damaging their credit necessarily, because part of the CARES Act is also that lenders cannot report the forbearance on a borrower's credit. Let's look at an example of someone getting a forbearance from their bank in April. It is now December, so they have gone eight months without making payments. So the bank does not necessarily report to the credit agencies that they're behind in payments because they're on this forbearance. But if they approach a mortgage officer or a mortgage lender and say, "Hey, I want to refinance my house to fix these arrears," the mortgage company may say, "Well, wait a minute, you're eight months behind. So we're not going to give you a loan because you're behind in your payments." It's not a credit issue, but the banks don't like doing what they're calling "foreclosure bailout loans." So it's not really a credit issue, but it does impact your ability to get a new loan.

What kind of strategies have you seen that are successful, in light of that?

Shawn Yesner: We go back to the typical loan modification. Some people on mortgage forbearances have hopefully saved some money and can get on a repayment plan to pay a lump sum down payment and a little more to catch up every month. That is where a Chapter 13 bankruptcy payment plan comes into play. At the end of the day, I'm starting to hear something called a forced sale. In the Great Recession of 2008 to 2014, a lot of people were short selling their homes. Well, now, many people have built up equity. If they are behind on their mortgage and can't figure out a way to catch up, they can sell their home, pull that cash out, rent for a little bit until their credit gets repaired, and then buy something else.

Do you anticipate a similar situation to the Great Recession of 2008 to 2014?

Shawn Yesner: I don't think it will be as big as that, but I do see something coming. I've seen a slight uptick in my practice regarding foreclosures and bankruptcies, but not the big wave that many of us in the industry are anticipating; that hasn't quite hit yet. Plus, now we're into the Thanksgiving and Christmas timeframe, and frankly, people just don't want to think about this stuff during the holidays.

If people are facing challenges and not quite sure what to do, how can you help them? What does it look like to work with you?

Shawn Yesner: There is one caveat; I'm a Florida licensed attorney. So I can certainly help but only here in Florida. If somebody outside of Florida has one of these issues, I would suggest they contact an attorney in their local area. I'll also take this opportunity to do a shameless plug. I do have a podcast that's called "Crushing Debt." It comes out every Thursday, and it's on Apple and all the other major podcast players. That gives a lot of generic information that people can use. I'm open to having conversations with people, but I can only provide legal advice for Florida issues. If you are in the Florida area, we always do a free case analysis, a 45 minute to 1-hour free consultation. We'll go over your mortgage debt, your unsecured debt, what kinds of credit cards you have, and what type of student loans, IRS debt, and medical bills you have. From there, we come up with an all-encompassing plan. Maybe bankruptcy is a bad idea, and loan modification is a good idea or vice versa. We don't use the same tool to fix every problem. We come up with a couple of options that are specific to that unique individual.

What inspired you to get into this line of work?

Shawn Yesner: I've wanted to be an attorney since high school. And it's a funny story. My father is a CPA, and most of the men and women in my family are professionals. I knew from an early age that I would be my own boss, I was going to own my business, and that I was going to do something beyond my undergrad degree. I took a law class my senior year in high school just to see if I enjoyed it or not. We had a mock trial in that class, and I was one of the plaintiff's attorneys and prepared a friend of mine to be the plaintiff's witness. We did the mock trial, and the teacher didn't pick me for the school's mock trial team, but she chose my witness that I had worked with and prepared for so long. I joke that out of spite, I said, "I'll show you," and ended up going to law school. I wanted to be a litigator. My undergrad degree was in accounting because of my dad, so I went into law school, thinking I would be an IRS attorney or something along those lines. I got bit by the litigation bug when I was in law school, but the first job that I had right after graduating was with a real estate attorney, so I became a dirt lawyer.

As a kid, I was bullied in school. In helping people defend themselves from foreclosure, credit card collections, garnishments, and the like, I discovered that I enjoy defending people from their "financial bullies." I enjoy the feeling of finishing a consultation and hearing my client say, "I feel like a weight has been lifted off my shoulders." or "I feel like I can finally get a good night's sleep."

For people who could benefit from your experience, how can they find and connect with you?

Shawn Yesner: The easiest way is my law firm's website, which is www.yesnerlaw.com. You can also listen to my podcast and read my two books. The first one is called "Crushing Debt: 9 Ways to Eliminate Financial Bullies." The book discusses many of the topics in this interview: foreclosure, loan modification, short sale, bankruptcy, debt settlement, IRS debt, student loan debt, etc. The second book is entitled "Become Debt Free in Less Than One Hour," and you can get that for free at www.shawnmyesner.com/becomedebtfree.

SHAWN M. YESNER, ESQ.

Attorney, Author, Podcaster

Yesner Law

Shawn M. Yesner is a Florida native, born in Tampa and raised in Miami. After graduating from Florida State University with a Bachelor of Science degree in Accounting, Shawn enrolled in the Cumberland School of Law, Samford University, graduating with a Juris Doctor (J.D.) Degree in 1998.

Prior to starting his own practice, Shawn was an associate attorney at one of Florida's largest lender foreclosure firms. In 2004, Shawn left the plaintiff's side of the practice to form a law firm focused on helping homeowners keep their homes or get rid of their homes while incurring minimal liability. After building a successful multi-practice firm, Shawn founded Yesner Law, P.L. in September 2012, again focusing on helping homeowners, consumers, and others eliminate the financial bullies in their lives.

Shawn has been a speaker at multiple Continuing Legal Education Seminars, Realtor® Education Seminars, and Networking Seminars, and has authored an article entitled Loan Modifications Can Help Borrowers Keep Their Homes as part of a book titled Florida Foreclosure: What Lawyers Need to Know Now published by Thomson Reuters in 2009.

In November 2015, "The Crushing Debt" Podcast was launched and can now be heard on Apple Podcasts, Spotify, Stitcher, Google, iHeartRadio, and all other podcast players. The podcast supports the law firm with the message that "everything will be okay." In September 2018, Shawn's book, Crushing Debt: 9 Strategies to Eliminate Financial Bullies was released and is available on Amazon.com. In September 2020, Shawn released his second book, Become Debt Free in Less Than One Hour, and is available for free at www.ShawnMYesner.com/BecomeDebtFree.

WEBSITES: www.yesnerlaw.com

www.shawnMYesner.com/BecomeDebtFree

EMAIL: Shawn@YesnerLaw.com

MARY ELLEN CIGANOVICH

MARY ELLEN CIGANOVICH

Conversation with Mary Ellen Ciganovich

Mary Ellen, you are an author, educator, and speaker. Tell us about your work and the people you serve.

Mary Ellen Ciganovich: I began my healing journey after coming through my own epilepsy and Multiple Sclerosis diagnosis. I was just learning to heal myself by utilizing my mind's power along with herbs, vitamins, meditation, visualization, exercise, and being aware of all the foods I put into my body. I wrote my first book, "Healing Words: Life Lessons to Inspire," and began posting a "Truth of the Day" as a way to promote "Healing Words." These "Truth of the Day" posts then became my second book, "T.R.U.T.H Taking Responsibility Unleashes True Healing." I then had many people asking me to assist them on their life journey. Since I taught middle school for over 15 years, it was natural to teach others the "healing" truths I learned. I have many clients that utilize my services. Some pay, some do work around my home, and others pay when they can. For me, I just want people to wake up, wake up to what they need to learn instead of always pointing a finger or blaming someone else. People usually say, "It's not my fault," or "___ made me do ___." The truth is, no one person makes you do anything you do not choose to do on some level! Why did you make that choice, and what do you need to learn from making that choice?

What are the most common challenges your clients face?

Mary Ellen Ciganovich: In our society right now, everyone is stuck in fear. Our societal teachings are so incorrect. We teach worry, anxiety, stress, fear; our society reinforces everything negative. We teach parents to worry about their children. If you have been a good parent, why should you worry about your kids? People are stuck in worry and fear about personal relationships not going well. Your relationships are a mirror for you! So, what do you need to learn about yourself? Everyone wants someone to love them, and this is impossible until you first love you! All relationships are a mirror for you, business or personal. I teach people that you can only come from one of two emotions: love or fear. When you come from a mindset of "fear," it is all negative with judgments, expectations, and motives. When you come from a "loving" mindset, it is positive, uplifting, and energizing with no judgments, expectations, or motives. You are simply there to assist the other person on their life journey. This philosophy has helped me heal my own life, and it is now what I teach to others.

What are some common mistakes people make to find themselves in these traps?

Mary Ellen Ciganovich: Number One: They are asleep.

Most people are afraid to "wake up" to their own God-given power to succeed and be happy. They were brought up in a home being told certain principles about life, which were probably false. Yet, instead of creating the life they really want, they recreate the "home situation" they didn't like, and the sad part is they do not even realize what they are doing!

Number Two: Refusal to wake up.

When I point this out, my client will agree with me, and instead of doing the work I prescribe to be free and create a life of peace and happiness, they choose to continue to stay stuck! Many people feel comfortable in their lives – even when it is not working for them.

How has the recent pandemic affected your business?

Mary Ellen Ciganovich: I've seen a surge in my business because people are finally beginning to understand the collective consciousness all of us have. I tell my clients to listen to the news to obtain the information they need to be safe. Then turn off that negativity. Anyone who listens to the news 24/7 will have turmoil inside. They begin taking this out on their spouse or their children. A great truth is, "You are never upset for the reason you think!" The person caught up in the "news negativity" will begin yelling at their family when they are upset about our countries' situation, and they feel helpless to do anything about it.

What inspired you to begin helping others?

Mary Ellen Ciganovich: When I was six years old, I was diagnosed with epilepsy. Even though I had a very mild case, I always felt different. I was told I was a mistake and not wanted. My self-esteem was very low growing up. Then in 1986, I was diagnosed with Multiple Sclerosis! I thought, "Okay, I went through epilepsy; I can handle this too." My life just kind of snowballed from one spot to another, and since I had no one to turn to, I had to learn to "heal" myself. My birth family was quite dysfunctional, and my first husband left right when I was diagnosed with Multiple Sclerosis (no, not because of it). I had to learn to get myself together; I learned how to get in touch with my God-given strength of "knowingness" to live peaceably. I am now married to my second husband for the last 23 years! You see, I could never have found Pete, my second husband if I had not learned to love myself first!

After marrying Pete, I wrote the first edition of "Healing Words: Life Lessons to Inspire." Every vignette in the book came to me from my Higher Power- God! I really did not want to write it, and God would not let me alone. To market "Healing Words: Life Lessons to Inspire," I began writing a "Truth of the Day." Now the "Truths" are the basis for my second book, " T.R.U.T.H Taking Responsibility Unleashes True Healing." My "Truth of the Day" posts have just gone into syndication with iHeartRadio, Conversations Live News, and WYAD-FM in Mississippi.

I want people to understand what truth is as people use the word "truth" incorrectly. Truth does not change. A truth can be based on a fact, and all facts are not a truth. You must look at yourself truthfully, which means you let your "ego-self" drop away. You take responsibility for your errors; you learn from them and go forward. When you do not learn from your mistakes, you doom yourself to commit them over and over again.

I genuinely love to see people's light bulbs turn on when they say, "Oh my gosh, you just said what I needed to hear." I've been there before, and I am so blessed to have so much peace in my life now! I want to assist somebody else.

How can people who resonate with your message find you and connect with you?

Mary Ellen Ciganovich: The best way is through my website at https://www.askmaryellen.com. All of my links are there, or you can just Google "Ask Mary Ellen," and I am sure you will find me. I do a podcast live on Facebook and Instagram every Monday called "Miracles with Mary Ellen." The episodes are then uploaded to my YouTube channel at "Ask Mary Ellen" or https://YouTube.com/Askmaryellen.

Both of my books are on Amazon, and links can be found at www.askmaryellen.com.

MARY ELLEN CIGANOVICH

Educator and Speaker

Author of "Healing Words: Life Lessons to Inspire"and "T.R.U.T.H. Taking Responsibility Unleashes True Healing"

Director of R.E.A.L. Health, Chattanooga, TN

Mary Ellen Ciganovich is a writer, speaker, educator, and author. She is Director of R.E.A.L Health in Chattanooga, Tennessee. Mary Ellen knows when you are "Really Enthusiastic About Life," you can live peaceably.

Mary Ellen began her healing journey as a child through dealing with a diagnosis of epilepsy as well as a very dysfunctional family. She went to the University of Georgia, obtaining her degree in Education. She is a proud mother to her daughter and has used her teaching skills to help children in many impoverished areas of the country.

Her first marriage ended and Mary Ellen became a single parent working mother. She then received a diagnosis of Multiple Sclerosis. While searching for healing, Mary Ellen turned to Spiritual Education classes at The Awareness Center of Atlanta. She studied all books of the Bible plus "A Course in Miracles" where she became aware of her healing power.

She remarried and moved to NC where she continued her healing studies at The Awakened Heart Center. Mary Ellen began studying Chinese herbs and other holistic healing practices.

Mary Ellen moved to Chattanooga, Tennessee. She began studying Ayurvedic healing to find ways to deal with Multiple Sclerosis. Mary Ellen learned many successful therapies for MS, from diet, exercise, herbs, and supplements to identifying her body type to utilize specific treatments.

She is the author of two books, "Healing Words: Life Lessons to Inspire" and "T.R.U.T.H Taking Responsibility Unleashes True Healing."

Are you tired of feeling let down and uninspired? Do you want to see your life differently? Are you a single parent or going through a divorce? Do you want to learn how to have peace in any relationship, or do you just want to learn how to wake up to feel empowered? Connect with Mary Ellen Ciganovich at www.askmaryellen.com. She will be happy to assist you with these issues and more.

LINKS: "Healing Words: Life Lessons to Inspire" on Amazon at https://www.amazon.com/dp/b08b33y8jd/

"T.R.U.T.H. Taking Responsibility Unleashes True Healing" on Amazon at https://www.amazon.com/dp/1728842883/

Remarkable Business

WEBSITE: https://www.askmaryellen.com

FACEBOOK: https://Facebook.com/Askmaryellen

TWITTER: https://twitter.com/askmaryellen

INSTAGRAM: https://Instagram.com/maryciganovich

LINKEDIN: https://LinkedIn.com/Maryellenciganovich

YOUTUBE: https://YouTube.com/Askmaryellen

GISELLE MASCARENHAS

GISELLE MASCARENHAS

Conversation with Giselle Mascarenhas

Giselle, you are a branding coach and the founder of Bold Instatute. Tell us about Bold Instatute and the types of people you help.

Giselle Mascarenhas: Bold Instatute is a space where we coach successful entrepreneurs who have yet to use Instagram as a tool to build their business. We take them on the journey to understand how to use it. Instagram is a very different animal. Professionals in their 40s, 50s, or 60s can be incredibly successful yet still find social media as an intimidating beast, and they hate to even think about having to learn something else. We take that overwhelming feeling away by giving them the tools they need to take advantage of this beautiful, amazing opportunity in their arena, with the world right at their fingertips.

What is the benefit of Instagram for business owners?

Giselle Mascarenhas: I want to put this in straightforward terms. The grid on Instagram is the magazine of your brand. People can go through it quickly and get a good idea of your values, who you are as a human, and your purpose-driven brand as a business. Then think of Instagram "stories" as the reality TV portion, where you let your hair down and allow people into your life so they can build a relationship with you. IGTV serves as your YouTube, where you can create your own show, including a series, episodes, or whatever you desire. Instagram Live is an arm to reach everyone that is connected to you and lets them know, "Hey, by the way, I'm here, and I'm having a conversation." Lastly, Instagram "reels" have just taken over and are blessing you by the thousands if you are engaging right now. Instagram is giving a lot of love to people doing reels. So it is just a fantastic array of facets to help you connect and build influence.

How do you explain the appeal of Instagram versus Facebook?

Giselle Mascarenhas: The Instagram audience goes in there to be entertained and escape. However, when they need to make a decision on something, they're now using that search engine. So don't take it for granted that it's just a visual tool. It's also somewhere where people are a little less wary of building and connecting. Facebook is taking a turn where it is very polarizing, and people are creating severe opinions on specific topics. Facebook is terrific when it comes to groups, but Instagram is where people feel comfortable. It's like a warm tea.

Do business owners that reach out to you already know the value of Instagram? Or are you finding that you need to educate them?

Giselle Mascarenhas: They really don't know. I first explain the value of Instagram and then go over mindset issues. Especially for people not born into social media, there are a lot of blocks there. It's my job to help people understand that they are in control. They can curate a community that is beautiful, thriving, engaging, and protected from the crap.

What are the common blocks or misconceptions people have when it comes to Instagram?

Giselle Mascarenhas: I do a show every Wednesday on Instagram Live at 2:00 pm central. Last week, this beautiful woman, Michelle Nance, who's been through my program, came on to share her experience. Nothing is ever staged, so I asked her, "What were your initial reservations about Instagram?" She said, "I felt like it was all fake. Why would I go on there and show pictures of my family or what I'm eating? Who does that?" I then asked, "After 12 weeks in the program, how do you feel about it?" She replied, "I just did a summit because you opened up my world to show me that my people are there. That is where I can actually connect in a way to build a relationship. In a short amount of time, she came in resistant and now sees the beautiful potential and the opportunities awaiting her. It's up to her...all she has to do is invest the time.

Can you give us a big picture of the steps you take people through in your program?

Giselle Mascarenhas: Everything I do is based on the five "C"s. If one is not there, none of it works. These can be applied to all social platforms. Number one is the "courage" to show up vulnerably. If you don't have the courage to show up, you will not build those relationships. The second "C" is "content." Your content must be engaging (evoke emotion), educational (tips and steps), and transformational (take people on a journey to solve a problem). The next one is "community." You have to invest in people by going to their accounts and giving them love and comments on their posts to get that back in return. The fourth "C" is "consistency." When you are just starting, commit to a certain number of times a week because the algorithms will bless you when you stay consistent. When you are ready to grow, and the consistent habits are already there, you can grow at an even faster pace. Consistency is everything. Last but not least is commitment.

You have to commit to yourself to show up and be there and to your followers to who you promised to give value and resources. In my program, we talk about using these 5 "C"s to build a thriving, awesome community that is not about vanity metrics. It's about value.

How do you help people get over their initial hesitation and shyness?

Giselle Mascarenhas: I honestly meet them where they're at. My program is very hands-on, and I don't care about serving 1,000 people a day. I care about helping that one person who is saying, "I know I need to do this, but I am petrified." Those feelings are real. So we take baby steps. I first teach people how to use "stories" because it disappears in 24 hours. If you are scared, turn that camera on, share a little bit about what you do, let the viewer know what is in it for them, and then let it go. Don't go back and rewatch it. Let it go, and then do it again the next day and the next day. Press the button, turn the camera on yourself, and realize that you didn't die and you also didn't kill anybody in the process.

What inspired you to create the Bold Instatute?

Giselle Mascarenhas: I think Covid has forced me to hone in on where my passion comes from. I'm passionate about extracting the magic from people and teaching them how to use it to connect to their tribe. But I think it started a long time ago when I wasn't feeling understood. People couldn't see me; they would just see the outer part of me. I'm very grateful to God that He gave me a beautiful, charismatic package on the outside, but when I was younger, that is all people saw. I just couldn't pierce that to show them there was more. Fast forward to today, and I see this generational gap. These amazing humans have so much wisdom to share, and they are intimidated and fearful of judgment. My job is to make them see they have complete control of being understood for who they are. That is where my passion comes from. The journey was a long one. I have always been an entrepreneur. I was a nightclub owner, and all I wanted to do was have people put their cares in my hands and make sure they had a great time. I was young and vibrant, so it worked. Then there was a natural progression to public relations. I became a publicist for big companies, and I did an excellent job, but it simply wasn't filling my soul. My soul is to extract magic from people and help them show up strong to build their community. Instagram is a place that feels like home to me. I understand it, and I want to teach people to do the same.

As a branding coach, what do you consider the keys to successful branding?

Giselle Mascarenhas: Branding is purpose-driven. The key to being able to share your purpose and having the courage to be vulnerable. It takes opening yourself up and allowing people in.

So the days of a curated Instagram where it's beautiful, everything matches, and it's all about a product or a service doesn't work anymore. That doesn't work anymore because people are coming on asking, "Why should I spend time with you? What are you offering me? What are your values? And what are you doing in the world to make it a better place?" It doesn't mean you have to go and hugely change the world. But you have to be intentional about what you are putting out there. People want to connect with more than just what you serve as a product. They want to see your values. You can do this by sharing your favorite restaurants, posting recipes, talking about your passion for fishing, or posting photos of your pets. It doesn't always have to be about a product. As a matter of fact, it should be the 80/20 rule when posting about your product or service. People want to know the person behind the brand. And that is really difficult for most people to do.

For people that would like more information about the Bold Instatute, how can they find you and connect with you?

Giselle Mascarenhas: First and foremost, download Instagram and then DM me at "the branding professor." That way, I know you already took that first step. You can also find me at boldinstatute.com. The site is ever-evolving since we have so much going on. If you DM me and want to learn more, I would love to do a strategy call. I believe in having conversations to understand your place on Instagram.

GISELLE MASCARENHAS

Branding Coach, Founder of Bold Instatute

Born and raised on South Texas's border, Giselle Mascarenhas-Villareal makes her living as an entrepreneur and personal branding coach. Her entrepreneurial journey began as a Nightclub owner from 2000-2009. She found herself doing the work of a publicist for several years for some of the high-profile individuals she met as a night-club owner and spent many years perfecting her process, building brands for high and low profile clients. Founding Indigo PR firm in 2013, Giselle was looking for a more accessible, affordable, and effective way to help people brand themselves. Over the next five years, the vast boom of social media and her passion for small business inspired her to modernize her idea of personal branding. With the immense untapped potential that social media presented, BOLD Insta-tute was born. Created for the entrepreneur, the focus of BOLD is to teach late-adapters to social media on how to show up authentically and consistently to build their influence, community, and business. Giselle teaches her students that you cannot "corporate" your way into people's hearts. Her numerous tips and tools explain that relatability and vulnerability are essential to building a fruitful and engaged social media community. Giselle continues to pursue her life's passion for helping others succeed by extracting their magic and purpose, actively redefining what it means to be a branding coach. Her unique perspective and talents have been featured in Yahoo Finance, Thrive Global, and Buzzfeed. Giselle teaches on a global scale, including the women's organization Femcity and has courses, programs, and tips at www.boldinstatute.com.

WEBSITES: www.boldinstatute.com

INSTAGRAM: https://www.instagram.com/thebrandingprofessor

MARSHA TERRY

MARSHA TERRY

Conversation with Marsha Terry

Marsha, you are a Mindset Coach from Mission, Texas. Tell us about your work and the people that you help.

Marsha Terry: My name says it all. I'm a Mindset Coach. I help people understand how their thoughts and words make them feel. Typically, I deal with women who feel invisible, like they are not being heard or seen. I teach them strategies to wake up **on** purpose **with** a purpose to master the entire day. I've coached real estate agents, financial advisors, and women that work in the judicial system. But that doesn't exclude the mother staying at home with her children, trying to juggle the realities of life. After all, we are all trying to do that, aren't we? Maybe you're a person who struggles with trying to figure out what your purpose is, or perhaps it's not even that complicated. Perhaps you're trying to decide whether or not you should go back to school as an adult learner; I can help you navigate to find the best decision for you. Some of my clients want help to find the confidence to use their voice with their spouse, partner, or boss without feeling like they're not heard or understood. I had a client who wanted to start a business but didn't have the confidence to do so. By our 3rd session, she had clarity and decided to move forward on it. It was remarkable to see her do that.

Do people already know they need to work on their mindset when they seek you out? Or do you need to create that awareness?

Marsha Terry: It's a little bit of both. Sometimes people know they need to change how they're thinking, but they don't know exactly what to do or where to start. And then you have the group of people that don't know they need to make a change. Someone may have said to me, "Hey, Marsha, I have a friend that I think could use your help." So, I see a mix of both categories. Generally, I can tell people need coaching by the language they use. It's a telltale sign. I grew up very shy and introverted. I hardly used to speak up for myself. But the value I discovered is learning to listen to people when they are talking. Many clients I coach are looking for a safe place where they feel like they are being heard. In this context and relationship, I help my clients recognize how their mindset has limited them from achieving the things they want. Most people don't pay attention to the words they use daily or in regular conversations. If you consistently say that you're broke and you don't have any money, then that is most likely who you are. Being aware of your words and thoughts affect who you get to become. It's the basis of the law of attraction as well as being biblical. Creating that awareness is the beginning of personal transformation.

Are there many misconceptions surrounding mindset?

Marsha Terry: Mindset is an industry word. I use the term "mindset" as a coach. But most people don't walk around saying to me, "Hey, Marsha, I need to change my mindset." So the misconception is found in that a lot of people never used to think about mindset. It's somewhat of a buzzword now. I believe it's a general feeling of really low energy, lacking the confidence to do the things you need or want to do, or not even knowing what you want to do. Some people feel very confused and overwhelmed. They need direction. These are things people share with me that indicate they are experiencing a mindset struggle. I think it's equally important to understand that mindset is tied to your beliefs. As Henry Ford stated, "Whether you can or you can't, you're right." What we believe about what we can or cannot do is directly tied to our mindset. So, when people have a shift in mindset, they also shift their belief system. It's almost like you get to rewire your brain. The end result is absolutely transformational!

What is one of the most common challenges your clients face, and what steps do you take them through to overcome this challenge?

Marsha Terry: Most people feel overwhelmed. I think that's the biggest thing that people come to me with. They don't know how to make a decision or get clarity on how to move forward in their life. So to help address this, I've created a program called "Masterful Morning." It's not revolutionary material; you can go out there and read a book on how to create a morning routine. But I've broken it down to how mindset really equates to your habits. If you can create a really solid habit in the morning, I believe that can set you up for the rest of your day. So we dive into determining what your habits are and whether or not you even have a morning routine. Why are these habits important to you? When you can intentionally grasp your morning, it changes everything about how you move through your day, your habits, and how you think. Ultimately, it changes how you show up in the world. And it changes what kind of results you get in your day. You might say to me, "Well, Marsha, I'm not a morning person, so this doesn't apply to me." My answer to that is simple: It's not so much that you have to get up at 5 am or 6 am to go through the process. What's important is that you develop the habit & accountability so that what you do sticks. Follow the proven system so you can get the mindset shift that you're looking for.

What are some common mistakes people make to sabotage themselves? How can improving mindset help to avoid these mistakes?

Marsha Terry: My mentor used to tell me all the time, "Marsha, you've got to get M.A.D." I was like, "What are you talking about?" He told me that "getting mad" was an acronym for: Make A Decision. So I share this with my clients all the time. Overwhelming feelings come from the inability to make a decision or stick to the decision you've decided to go through with. Knowing the end result of a decision isn't always relevant. What's important is making the decision first. And then once you make the decision, we can dive deeper into, "Okay, well, what is the next step? What happens after that?" The second step is to set yourself up for success. When you do, follow-through is inevitable. When you make the decision, you set yourself up so that you're able to execute it. The result over time is that you'll begin to shift how you think, how you do things, and how you speak. I had a client who was afraid of making cold calls; she got nervous, her stomach would be in knots. I explained to her the power and value of doing things we fear first thing in the morning. That way, she didn't spend her whole day agonizing over it. She also recognized that all she was doing was collecting answers: either YES or NO. In addition to that, she realized that if a client said "no" to her, it likely had nothing to do with her personally. We sabotage our efforts when we become so attached to the outcome instead of focusing on the steps to get from point A to point B. If we focus on the process, the outcome will take care of itself.

What inspired you to get into this field of work?

Marsh Terry: Professionally, I'm a registered nurse. I've been a nurse for over 30 years, and as much as it is a gratifying profession, it wasn't my passion. About ten years ago, I was very heavily involved in the network marketing industry, and I had an amazing mentor. I was always very intrigued by how he could ask questions and get people to move from point A to point B. So that was part of my inspiration. I wanted to learn how to ask people better questions and help them move into action. It was really rewarding to see somebody make a decision on how to change their life, their income, or positively impact their family. That inspired me to want to do the same thing for other people. My inspiration also comes from my own personal transformation. I used to be very quiet, shy, and reserved. Public speaking wasn't a thing I ever saw myself doing. However, that industry pushed me to be a presenter or a trainer. This meant speaking to groups of people, some who I knew, but mostly who I didn't know. This went against everything I felt on the inside. It made me nervous, and I never felt like I was good enough. Being in the spotlight just wasn't my thing. My mentors encouraged me to read books that deepened my awareness. One of those books is the "Four Agreements" by Don Miguel Ruiz. It's a book that I read back then and continue to read at the start of every year to get my mindset right, and it helps keep me self-aware. Once I was clear on being a coach, I also thought it was important to obtain certification in the industry. It's not required, but I wanted to do that for my own personal gratification. So I'm certified as a health and a life coach.

Is there anything else you would like to share?

Marsha Terry: Over the last few years, I've learned to wake up every day and exercise some self-compassion. I think this is really important. There is so much going on in the world that you can easily get overwhelmed with things you can't control. Also, there's so much negativity that we're exposed to daily. The news is negative; social media can be negative, never mind having to deal with everyday life challenges. Anxiety, worry, and overwhelm are so common. So, being kind to yourself first thing in the morning is crucial. You can say affirmations, which move you into action and change your thinking. Perhaps you can read a book that speaks to you or listen to something that energizes you. Be kind to yourself. Feed your mind, body, and soul before anything or anyone else. Give yourself some grace & space to make mistakes. Pace yourself in everything that you do. Doing this helps you have more meaningful and intentional connections with the people around you. Overall, you'll be a happier person. Who doesn't want to be around a happy person?

How can people find you, connect with you, and learn more?

Marsha Terry: Join my Masterful Mornings Facebook group to connect with me and others in my community. Secondly, my website www.marshaterry.com is where you can find my free workbook, "Masterful Morning," that you can download along with other resources.

MARSHA TERRY, RN MSN CMOM CLC

Mindset Coach

Marsha Terry is a Canadian-born Registered Nurse with her Master's in Science in Nursing focusing on Leadership and Management. She is the Administrator at both of Terry Physical Therapy's locations.

Her passion for leadership is further exemplified as a Mindset Transformational Coach. As a mindset coach, Marsha intimately understands the importance of practicing a morning routine. She has developed a workbook called "Masterful Mornings," which gives her clients a practical up-leveling to morning routines. In addition to this, she also provides individual coaching sessions. In her 12-session customized program, "The Mindset Shift," her clients gain clarity, discover personal work-life balance and develop a greater sense of self-awareness. Her clients leave her sessions feeling rejuvenated.

When she's not hanging out with her husband and two boys in South Texas, you'll find Marsha active in her community, especially with Village in the Valley (ViVA), a non-profit organization of which she is a co-founder.

In her leisure time, she enjoys feeding her culinary skill. Her Canadian and Jamaican heritage allows her to blend culture and food with her family. Follow Marsha Terry on Facebook or

@TheMindsetTransformer on Instagram to get to know her personally. You can also join her Facebook group https://www.facebook.com/groups/masterfulmornings to be supported in your morning practice.

WEBSITE: www.marshaterry.com

FACEBOOK: https://www.facebook.com/groups/masterfulmornings

INSTAGRAM: https://www.instagram.com/themindsettransformer/

LINKEDIN: https://www.linkedin.com/in/marshaterrymindsetcoach/

ABOUT THE PUBLISHER

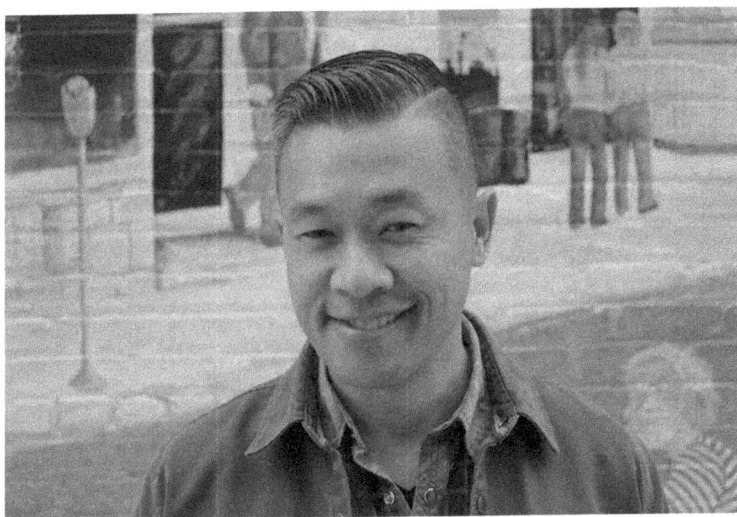

Mark Imperial is a Best-Selling Author, Syndicated Business Columnist, Syndicated Radio Host, and internationally recognized Stage, Screen, and Radio Host of numerous business shows spotlighting leading experts, entrepreneurs, and business celebrities.

His passion is to discover noteworthy business owners, professionals, experts, and leaders who do great work and share their stories and secrets to their success with the world on his syndicated radio program titled "Remarkable Radio."

Mark is also the media marketing strategist and voice for some of the world's most famous brands. You can hear his voice over the airwaves weekly on Chicago radio and worldwide on iHeart Radio.

Mark is a Karate black belt, teaches kickboxing, loves Thai food, House Music, and his favorite TV shows are infomercials.

Learn more:

www.MarkImperial.com
www.ImperialAction.com
www.RemarkableRadioShow.com

www.ingramcontent.com/pod-product-compliance
Lightning Source LLC
Chambersburg PA
CBHW071603200326
41519CB00021BB/6853